Contents

All bears 6

Most bears 12

Some bears 14

Every bear 20

Bear facts 22

Picture glossary 23

Index 24

There are many types of animals.

Creature Comparisons

Bears

Tracey Crawford

Heinemann LIBRARY

www.heinemann.co.uk/library
Visit our website to find out more information about Heinemann Library books.

To order:
 Phone 44 (0) 1865 888066
Send a fax to 44 (0) 1865 314091
 Visit the Heinemann Bookshop at www.heinemann.co.uk/library to browse our
catalogue and order online.

First published in Great Britain by Heinemann Library,
Halley Court, Jordan Hill, Oxford OX2 8EJ, part of Harcourt
Education. Heinemann is a registered trademark of Harcourt
Education Ltd.

Editorial: Tracey Crawford, Cassie Mayer, Dan Nunn,
and Sarah Chappelow
Design: Jo Hinton-Malivoire
Picture Research: Tracy Cummins and Tracey Engel
Production: Duncan Gilbert

Originated by Chroma Graphics (Overseas) Pte. Ltd
Printed and bound in China by South China
Printing Company

ISBN 978 0 431 18226 1 (hardback)
11 10 09 08 07
10 9 8 7 6 5 4 3 2 1

ISBN 978 0 431 18349 7 (paperback)
12 11 10 09 08
10 9 8 7 6 5 4 3 2 1

British Library Cataloguing in Publication Data
Crawford, Tracey
    Bears. - (Creature comparisons)
    1.Bears - Juvenile literature
    I.Title
    599.7'8

Acknowledgements
The publishers would like to thank the following for permission
to reproduce photographs: Alamy pp. 9 (John Schwieder), 10
(Garry DeLong), 13 (Balan), 17 (Winston Fraser); Corbis pp. 4
(bird, Arthur Morris), 5 (A. & S. Carey/zefa), 7 (Gunter Marx
Photography), 14 (Ralph A. Clevenger), 15 (Keren Su), 18 (Michael
DeYoung), 22 (polar bear, David E. Myers/zefa); Howie Garber
p. 19; Getty Images pp. 4 (fish), 6 (PhotoDisc), 11 (Roy Toft), 16
(Andy Rouse), 20 (Eastcott Momatiuk), 21 (Hans Strand); Naturepl.
com p. 12; Science Photo Library p. 22 (Sun bear, Art Wolfe);
Carlton Ward p. 4 (snake, frog).

Cover photograph of a giant panda reproduced with permission
of Corbis/Tim Davis and a brown bear reproduced with permission
of Corbis/Royalty Free. Back cover photograph of a polar bear
reproduced with permission of Corbis/Michael DeYoung.

Every effort has been made to contact copyright holders of any
material reproduced in this book. Any omissions will be rectified in
subsequent printings if notice is given to the publishers.

Bears are one type of animal.

Bears are mammals.

All bears have fur.

All bears have paws and claws.

backbone

All bears have a backbone.

All baby bears get milk from
their mother.

All bears walk on four legs.

All bears can stand on two feet.

Most bears sleep during the winter.

But this bear does not.

Some bears eat fish.

But these bears do not.

Some bears are big.

Some bears are small.

Some bears swim.

Some bears climb.

Every bear is different.

Every bear is special.

Bear facts

Polar bears have two layers of fur. This helps keep them warm.

Sun bears spend most of their time in trees. They have long claws. This helps them climb.

Picture glossary

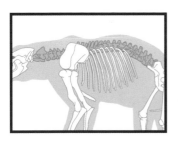 **backbone** the part of the skeleton that goes from the head to the tail

Index

backbone 8, 23   fur 6

claw 7   paw 7

fish 14

Notes to parents and teachers
Before reading
Talk to the children about bears. Has anyone seen a bear on television or in a zoo? Have they got a favourite teddy bear?

After reading
Share the tale "We're going on a bear hunt", joining in with actions, e.g. Swish swash through the water; Squelch, squelch through the mud, etc. Play the Bear Circle game. Tell the children to sit in a circle facing inwards. Give each child a name of a bear, either brown bear, grizzly bear, or polar bear. Call out one of the bears and those children stand up and move outside the circle. On command they move around the circle in a given direction e.g. crawl, lumber, and run. On the command "Into the cave", they race back to their places and sit down.
Draw a large outline of a bear on a large sheet of brown paper and cut it out. Cover the bear with scrunched square of brown tissue paper. Use black scrunched tissue paper for the eyes and mouth and a large bead painted black for the nose.

24